BIRTH AND DEATH OF A CITY

Elizabeth Raum

www.raintreepublishers.co.uk
Visit our website to find out more information about **Raintree** books.

To order:
☎ Phone 44 (0) 1865 888112
📄 Send a fax to 44 (0) 1865 314091
💻 Visit the Raintree bookshop at **www.raintreepublishers.co.uk** to browse our catalogue and order online.

First published in Great Britain by Raintree,
Halley Court, Jordan Hill, Oxford OX2 8EJ,
part of Harcourt Education.
Raintree is a registered trademark of
Harcourt Education Ltd.

© Harcourt Education Ltd 2007
First published in paperback in 2007
The moral right of the proprietor has been asserted.

Editorial: Louise Galpine and Catherine Veitch
Design: Michelle Lisseter and Bridge Creative Services
Illustrations: Bridge Creative Services
Picture Research: Hannah Taylor and Fiona Orbell
Production: Camilla Crask

Originated by Modern Age
Printed and bound in China by WKT Company
Limited

10 digit ISBN 1 406 20480 3 (hardback)
13 digit ISBN 978 1 4062 0480 3
11 10 09 08 07
10 9 8 7 6 5 4 3 2 1

10 digit ISBN 1 406 20505 2 (paperback)
13 digit ISBN 978 1 4062 0505 3
11 10 09 08 07
10 9 8 7 6 5 4 3 2 1

Library of Congress Cataloging-in-Publication Data
Raum, Elizabeth
Birth and death of a city. - (Fusion)
307.1'4
A full catalogue record for this book is available from
the British Library.

Acknowledgements
The author and publisher are grateful to the
following for permission to reproduce copyright
material: Art Resource/NY (The New York Public
Library) pp. **10–11**; Corbis p. **13** inset (Bettmann),
16–17 (Bettmann), **18–19** (Bettmann) **5** (Galen
Rowell); Corbis/Royalty Free p. **6**; Corbis/
Schenectady Museum: Hall of Electrical History
Foundation pp. **22–23**; Courtesy of California State
Parks 2006 p. **4**; Getty Images pp. **26–27** (Justin
Sullivan); Getty Images/Hulton Archive p. **25**; San
Francisco History Center, San Francisco Public
Library p. **21**; The Bancroft Library pp. **8–9**,
12–13, **15**.

Cover photograph of San Francisco earthquake
damage reproduced with permission of California
Historical Society (FN-16826).

Every effort has been made to contact copyright
holders of any material reproduced in this book. Any
omissions will be rectified in subsequent printings if
notice is given to the publishers.

The publishers would like to thank Nancy Harris and
Daniel Block for their assistance with the preparation
of this book.

Disclaimer
All the Internet addresses (URLs) given in this book
were valid at the time of going to press. However,
due to the dynamic nature of the Internet, some
addresses may have changed, or sites may have
changed or ceased to exist since publication. While
the author and publishers regret any inconvenience
this may cause readers, no responsibility for any
such changes can be accepted by either the author
or the publishers.

It is recommended that adults supervise children on
the Internet.

Contents

Some words are printed in bold, **like this**. You can find out what they mean on page 30. You can also look in the box at the bottom of the page where they first appear.

Ghost town

Bodie is in California, in the United States of America. Bodie is a **ghost town**. This means it was once a busy town, but no one lives there now. Buildings are falling down. Grass grows in the streets. What happened to Bodie? Why was the city born? Why did it die?

In 1859, William Bodey discovered (found) gold in the area. People rushed to Bodie to dig for gold. They were called **miners**. People set up shops. The shops sold supplies to miners.

This is how ▼ Bodie looked in the 1880s.

ghost town   once-lively town that is now empty
miner   person who digs for gold or other natural substances

Bodie was a lively place. There were places to eat, drink, and have fun. The town had a bank full of gold. By 1880, Bodie had 10,000 people. Most of them were miners.

When the gold ran out, people left. Banks closed. So did shops. Only empty buildings remained. Bodie became a ghost town. People lived in Bodie for less than 100 years.

▼ This is how Bodie looks today.

A city that lived on

The city of San Francisco is also in California. San Francisco is 400 kilometres (250 miles) west of Bodie (see map on page 7). The city has had a long life.

Bodie's **population** is now zero. No one lives in Bodie. San Francisco has 744,000 people. People from all over the world visit San Francisco. Why did one town live and the other die?

This is San ▶
Francisco today.

6

population   number of people who live in a place

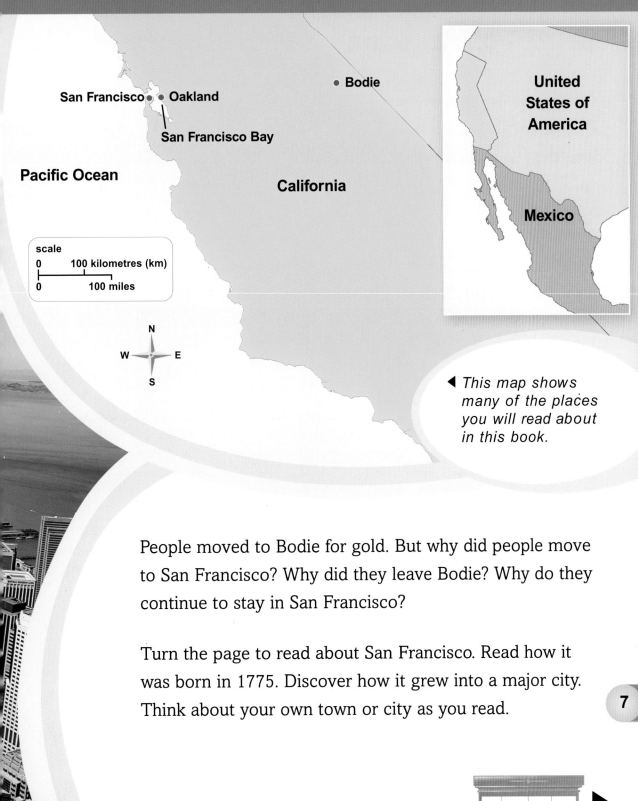

San Francisco ● ● Oakland

San Francisco Bay

Pacific Ocean

California

● Bodie

United States of America

Mexico

scale
0   100 kilometres (km)
0   100 miles

N
W ← → E
S

◀ This map shows many of the places you will read about in this book.

People moved to Bodie for gold. But why did people move to San Francisco? Why did they leave Bodie? Why do they continue to stay in San Francisco?

Turn the page to read about San Francisco. Read how it was born in 1775. Discover how it grew into a major city. Think about your own town or city as you read.

1 7 7 5 ▶

Birth of a town

The first ship sailed into San Francisco **Bay** in 1775.
A bay is a place where the sea curves towards the land.
People saw that it was a good place for a town. The
weather was mild. The soil was good for farming. Ships
could land safely in the boat-landing area called
a **harbour**. It would be easy to buy and sell goods.

This church is called ▶
Mission Dolores. It was
built in 1776. It is
the oldest building in
San Francisco.

bay	place where the sea curves towards the land
harbour	place to land boats
settler	person who sets up a house and lives in a new place

Several Native American families already lived in the area. They grew vegetables. They fished and hunted. They lived in small villages. They moved around a lot.

New **settlers** started to move to San Francisco Bay in 1776 (see map on page 7). Settlers are people who set up a home in a new place. The first settlers came from Mexico.

Think about your own town or city. Was there farming, hunting, or fishing there? How did early settlers arrive?

1835 ▶

Yerba Buena

In 1835, William Richardson sailed into San Francisco **Bay**. He was a ship captain. He liked the area. He built a house there.

Other **settlers** followed. They named the new **settlement** (community) Yerba Buena. This is Spanish for "good herbs". The first settlers opened shops. They were called **trading posts**. They bought furs from trappers. They sold supplies. Yerba Buena belonged to Mexico.

Ships sailed into the **harbour**. They took the furs to market. After only twelve years, 400 people lived in Yerba Buena.

In 1847, the San Francisco Bay area became part of the United States of America. The new settlers elected a mayor (city leader). They changed the town's name. They named it San Francisco, after the name of the bay.

This drawing shows San Francisco ▶
in 1847. Ships have come to trade.
There are trading posts near the
water. There is a hotel and a school.
You can also see many homes.

settlement   new community
trading post   shop where goods are traded

City of Gold

In 1848, **miners** found gold in the California hills. People came from all over the world to dig for gold.

San Francisco's **population** grew. It grew from 400 to 20,000 people in only three years. There was plenty of work in San Francisco. It became known as the City of Gold. But there were not enough houses. Many people lived in tents.

At first, some ▼
settlers lived
in tents.

Gold rush prices

*A **gold rush** is a time when people move to an area to find gold. So many people arrived in San Francisco in 1848 that shops ran out of supplies. During the gold rush in California, one shop owner charged £25 for a shovel. In those days, £25 would buy what £500 buys today!*

Between 1849 and 1851, six fires swept through San Francisco. Tents and wooden houses burned easily. In 1851, one fire burned 1,500 homes. People rebuilt the houses out of stone and brick. San Francisco kept on growing.

About ten years later, the town of Bodie began. Gold drew people there, too. Bodie is 400 kilometres (250 miles) east of San Francisco.

Books and posters ▶ told about the discovery of gold.

AN ACCOUNT OF
CALIFORNIA,
AND THE
WONDERFUL GOLD REGIONS.

A New Arrival at the Gold Diggings.

WITH A DESCRIPTION OF
The Different Routes to California;
Information about the Country, and the Ancient and Modern Discoveries of Gold;
How to Test Precious Metals; Accounts of Gold Hunters;
TOGETHER WITH MUCH OTHER
Useful Reading for those going to California, or having Friends there.
ILLUSTRATED WITH MAPS AND ENGRAVINGS.

BOSTON:
PUBLISHED BY J. B. HALL, 66 CORNHILL.
For Sale at Skinner's Publication Rooms, 60½ Cornhill.

Price, 12½ cents.

1 8 6 9 ▶

Boomtown

San Francisco grew so fast that people called it a **boomtown**. New **settlers** arrived every day. People built more houses. They built more shops, banks, hotels, and schools.

Most of San Francisco's settlers and supplies arrived by ship. The boat trip from New York City to San Francisco often took six months. A **transcontinental railway** was being built. It crossed the United States from one coast to the other. The trip only took one week. City leaders wanted the railway to reach San Francisco.

The railway opened in 1869. It did not go all the way to San Francisco. The men who built the railway were from nearby Oakland, California. They made the train stop there. Oakland became a major shipping and rail centre. Even so, San Francisco continued to grow.

Bodie was booming, too. The **miners** who lived there looked for gold.

Building boom

In 1864, over 1,000 new buildings were built in San Francisco.

boomtown   town that grows quickly
transcontinental railway   train that crosses a continent

On May 10, 1869, workers finished building the transcontinental railway.

1 8 8 0 ▶

Different voices

As San Francisco grew, more people arrived. They came
from many different countries. Thousands of people came
from China. Many Chinese people got jobs building the
railway. They spoke a different language. They brought
new foods and music. They set up homes and shops.
They called the area they lived in Chinatown.

Many people welcomed the Chinese workers. But some
did not. Some Chinese workers were attacked. Some
Chinese workers were even killed. It took years for the
Chinese to feel at home in San Francisco.

*Many Chinese people ▶
moved to San Francisco.
They set up shops and
worked on the railway.*

Over the years, many different kinds of people moved there. They have made San Francisco a more interesting place. New **settlers** bring new ways. They also bring new ideas. Some of these new ideas become part of the city's way of life. The new settlers changed, too. They learned to live in their new community.

Chinese workers moved to Bodie, too. They helped build the railway. Some were **miners**. Miners are people who dig for gold. By 1880, around 10,000 people lived in Bodie.

1 8 9 0 ▶

Cable cars

In San Francisco's early days, people walked. They also rode in horse-drawn buses. San Francisco is very hilly. The horses had trouble pulling their heavy loads up the hills. There were accidents. The city was growing. It needed a new way for people to travel. San Francisco needed a **transportation system** or way of travelling.

In 1873, the first **cable car** began running in San Francisco. Cable cars run on tracks. A big cable runs beneath the streets. The cable pulls the cars along. Cable cars were faster and safer than horse-drawn buses. By 1890, San Francisco had more than 600 cable cars. People built houses along the cable car lines.

San Francisco had found a good way for people to travel within the city. Every large town or city needs a transportation system. What kinds of transportation do people use in your community?

cable car   special car pulled by a heavy wire rope

▼ San Francisco's cable cars are world-famous.

19

1906 ▶

Facing disaster

In 1892, Bodie had a terrible fire. The gold **mines** closed.
By 1906, people began leaving Bodie. They went to find
work in other places.

On April 18, 1906, there was an **earthquake** in San
Francisco. An earthquake causes the earth to shake.
Many buildings fell down.

Later that morning, fires broke out around the city. The
fires grew and grew. The fire department could not put
them out. Five hundred people died in the fires. Two out
of every three people lost their homes in the **disaster**.

San Francisco did not give up. People wanted to rebuild
the city. People all over the United States and the world
sent money. Clean-up crews and builders began work.
San Francisco was born again.

Not everyone stayed. Some families moved across the
bay to Oakland. Some people moved to other nearby
towns and cities.

disaster	something that causes damage, such as a fire, flood, or earthquake
earthquake	shaking or trembling of the earth
mine	place deep in the earth where people dig for gold and other natural substances

▼ These men are fixing sewer pipes after the earthquake of 1906.

21

1915 ▶

1915 celebration

Rebuilding San Francisco was a lot of work. People wanted the new San Francisco to be safe from fires and **earthquakes**.

By 1910, San Francisco was ready to celebrate. The 1915 World's Fair was to be held in San Francisco. People from all over the world visit a World's Fair. They go to see new products. They go to learn about new places.

San Francisco set aside land near the **harbour** for the fair buildings. The fair lasted more than nine months. Millions of people from all over the world visited San Francisco. They rode in **cable cars**. They shopped. They stayed in hotels. **Tourists** (visitors) saw an exciting, new San Francisco.

Millions of people ▶ visited the San Francisco World's Fair in 1915.

tourist visitor

Tourists help a city by spending money. They stay at hotels. They eat meals and buy products. If they have a good time, they tell their friends to visit.

1930 ▶

Leaving the city behind

By 1930, more than 634,000 people lived in San Francisco. San Francisco was running out of room. There was water on three sides of the city. Hills were on the fourth. People looked for new places to live.

San Francisco built two new bridges. In 1936, the San Francisco-Oakland **Bay** Bridge was opened. The Golden Gate Bridge was opened in 1937. The bridges connected San Francisco to other towns across the water.

Many people moved to nearby towns. They could **commute** or travel back and forth into the city.

The towns and cities near San Francisco grew. Other people found work in these new communities.

San Francisco became the centre of the San Francisco Bay area. This area is made up of many towns and cities. People built colleges and hospitals. They built new businesses. The whole area continued to grow.

But by the 1930s, Bodie was a **ghost town**. No one lived there.

commute   travel back and forth between a city and towns further away

▼ *This is the Golden Gate Bridge.*

TODAY ▶

In 2000, around 6.7 million people lived in the San Francisco Bay area.

San Francisco today

In the 1960s, San Francisco became home to poets and writers. Artists and musicians moved there, too. They thought San Francisco was beautiful. People came to the city to go to concerts and plays.

San Francisco was getting old. There were newer cities nearby. San Francisco's leaders were afraid that people would move away. They decided to fix up the old buildings. They put up modern flats. They built new office buildings. Many people and businesses stayed in the city. Also, other people and businesses moved there.

Today, people still move to San Francisco from all over the country and the world.

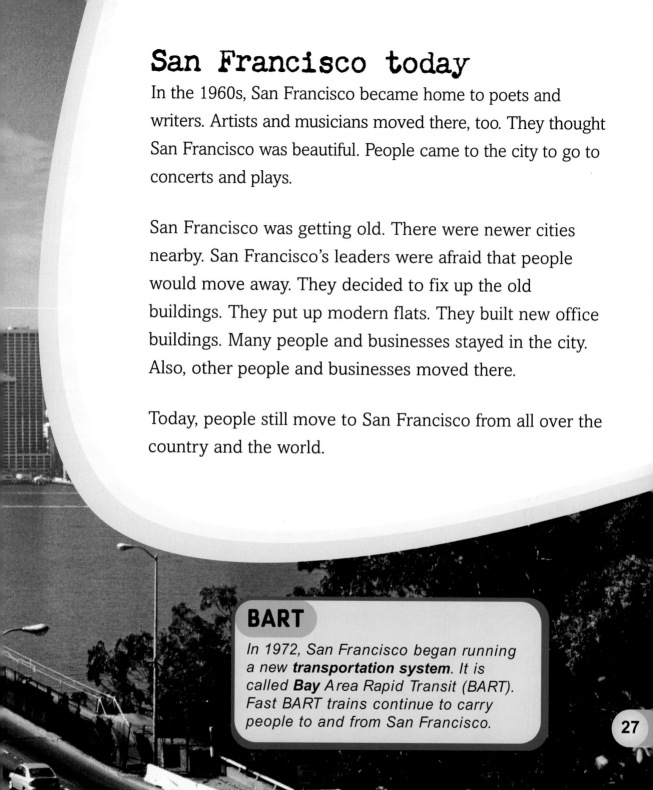

BART

In 1972, San Francisco began running a new **transportation system**. It is called **Bay** Area Rapid Transit (BART). Fast BART trains continue to carry people to and from San Francisco.

The life of a city

Look at how San Francisco has grown.

First stop, 1775
First ship arrives

Population unknown

Second stop, 1835
Early settlement

Population about 400

Third stop, 1848
Gold rush

Population about 20,000

Fourth stop, 1869
Boomtown

Population 149,473

Fifth stop, 1880
Chinese settlers

This is a timeline for San Francisco. Can you make one for your city? ▶

Sixth stop, 1890
Cable cars

Population 298,997

Seventh stop, 1906
Earthquake

Population about 350,000

Eighth stop, 1915
World's Fair

Population about 500,000

Ninth stop, 1930
People move to new
towns outside the city

Population 634,394

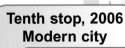
Tenth stop, 2006
Modern city

Population about 744,000

Glossary

bay place where the sea curves towards the land. San Francisco is located on a bay.

boomtown town that grows quickly. Bodie was a boomtown.

cable car special car pulled by a heavy wire rope. Cable cars still run in San Francisco.

commute travel back and forth between a city and towns further away. People often commute to work.

disaster something that causes damage, such as a fire, flood, or earthquake. San Francisco's earthquake was a disaster.

earthquake shaking or trembling of the earth. The San Francisco earthquake knocked down houses.

ghost town once-lively town that is now empty. Bodie is one of many California ghost towns.

gold rush time when people move to an area to find gold. California's gold rush began in 1848.

harbour place to land boats. San Francisco's harbour is crowded with boats.

mine place deep in the earth where people dig for gold and other natural substances. There were many mines in Bodie.

miner person who digs for gold or other natural substances. Bodie's first settlers were miners.

population number of people who live in a place. The population of San Francisco grew during the gold rush.

settlement new community. Every town or city began as a small settlement.

settler person who sets up a house and lives in a new place. It is not easy to be the first settler in a new place.

tourist visitor. Tourists enjoy riding cable cars in San Francisco.

trading post shop where goods are traded. The first settlers set up trading posts.

transcontinental railway train that crosses a continent. Chinese workers helped to build the transcontinental railway in the United States of America.

transportation system way of travelling. Every city needs a good transportation system.

Want to know more?

Books to read

- *The Living Town*, Nigel Hester (Franklin Watts, 2004)
- *Living in Cities*, Neil Morris (Franklin Watts, 2004)
- *A City Through Time*, Philip Steele, Steve Noon (Dorling Kindersley, 2004)

Websites

- Learn more about the California gold rush at this site: www.museumca.org/goldrush
- Go on an adventure and discover a lost city: www.bbc.co.uk/schools/indusvalley/

What will happen in the future if we run out of fuel and cannot make enough electricity? Find out in *The Future: Bleak or Bright?*

Find your way around Earth's landforms, cities, and roads in *Lost!* There is a catch. You will only have a few maps, a ruler, and a compass. You will have your brainpower, too!

Index